BY MEANS OF DEATH

GOOD FRIDAY MEDITATIONS

By Means Of Death

HUGHELL E. W. FOSBROKE

Foreword by the Rt. Rev. Henry Knox Sherrill

GREENWICH · CONNECTICUT

*T*o my fellow witnesses to the Gospel of "Jesus Christ, and him crucified," in the glad knowledge that, as in our meditation upon the Words of the Cross we reverently enter into the mind and heart of our Lord, we are drawn into closer union, one with another, in the saving power of his life laid down.

FOREWORD

$\mathcal{I}$t is with
deep gratification that I write this brief foreword to Dean Fosbroke's Good Friday meditations. Over forty years ago, at the Episcopal Theological School, I studied under him.
(I hope that at this late date he will not
object unduly to the word "studied.")

Through all the years since, his friendship
has been a source of inspiration and of
strength. As Professor at Nashotah House
and at the Episcopal Theological School and
for thirty years as Dean of the General
Theological Seminary, he has touched with
unusual power the minds and the hearts of
many young men preparing for the ministry.
Today his former students may be found in
positions of influence throughout the Church

at home and abroad. I know how greatly they will welcome these written words. But I am equally certain that a far larger constituency of thoughtful men and women will find in these pages a source of spiritual understanding. There have been many Good Friday books published. But here is a message which is unusual and distinctive. I venture to suggest that all those who must preach on Good Friday will find this book deeply suggestive for their own meditations.

The Dean emphasizes the Majesty and the Glory of the Eternal God. His equal insistence is that God in Christ does not stoop down from above but operates "within the process of human life, charging it with strange new possibilities of achievement."

To those of us who have been privileged to know Dean Fosbroke well, this book will have additional weight. For we know that this is more than a book; it is the Faith by which he lives.

HENRY KNOX SHERRILL

MEDITATIONS

One

$\mathcal{A}$mong the many portrayals of the crucifixion of our Lord, there is, perhaps, none more striking than that of the artist and mystic, William Blake. All is dark, in Blake's portrayal, except for one thin ray of sunlight that is just sufficient to reveal Jesus on the cross and, at the foot of the cross, a naked figure standing with arms outstretched and look fixed upward, in piteous longing, on the Christ. So the artist vividly interprets the great saying of the Christ: "I, if I be lifted up from the earth, will draw all men unto me."

Today as we gather—as all over the world groups of Christian people are gathering—to meditate upon the passion and death of our Lord, we may feel ourselves one, not only with the great company of Christian folk in every land, but one with all those for whom Christ died—one with a world which, in this generation, as perhaps never before, is all unconsciously lifting hands of groping need Godward.

For the time being, at any rate, we are not simply separate individuals; nor even a group set apart in contented relief that we are not too deeply involved in the terrible sense of insecurity, the corroding unhappiness, and the hopeless resignation that is the lot of so many millions of bewildered souls. But we are prepared, quietly and courageously, to realize that our lives are indissolubly bound up with theirs and to find that we are sharing in the perplexities and the pitiful distress of all God's children. We can even recall times when we also experienced their strange feeling of being caught up inescapably in the grasp of forces infinitely beyond human control.

But as we look at Jesus dying upon his cross, identifying himself to the full with our human struggle, our human failure, and our crippling sense of defeat, we know that, from the very heart of the mysterious power that maintains our world in being, there is being poured into human life, at its point of sorest need, the quickening energy of the living God, which brings triumph out of failure, victory out of defeat, life out of death.

For against the background of innocent suffering with which we have been sadly familiar, the figure upon the cross shines with an unearthly radiance. All the worst that man can do to man was inflicted upon Jesus: the devilish malignity of religious leaders who would stop at nothing in maintaining their own privileged position; the fumbling cowardice of Pilate, the time-serving governor; the blood lust of the mob; the callous brutality of the soldiers—all finding their cruel satisfaction in the suffering and death of one whose whole life had been devoted, in loving ministry, to human need.

But as we gaze, it is not pity that we feel but a profound reverence, for there on Calvary is the great turning point in the course of human affairs. And it is not simply that there the ideals of compassionate love which man had only dimly glimpsed before have come to stand out clearly and vividly with universal appeal. For witness what, in spite of the pitiable failure to live up to its aspiration, the trying to follow the example of Jesus has meant in history. "There can be no doubt," declares one of the most distinguished philosophers of our time, "as to what elements in the record have evoked a response from all that is best in human nature. The mother, the child and the bare manger, the lonely man homeless and self-forgetful, with his message of peace, love, and sympathy, the suffering, the agony, the tender words as life ebbed, the final despair, and the whole with the authority of supreme victory." [1]

Let us note particularly the phrase, "the authority of supreme victory." The Christ upon the cross is not just a victim of men's cruelty upon whom we can lavish our pity. He is actively engaged in the fulfillment of his Father's will, and so it is the loving energy of God Himself that is revealed in his patient acceptance of the worst that man can do. "God in Christ reconciling the world unto himself."

The deathless power embodied in the life of Jesus is, through his dying in loving union with his Father's will, triumphantly released into the whole process of human living: not only in the lives of apostles,

[1] Alfred N. Whitehead, *Adventures of Ideas* (New York: Macmillan, 1933), p. 214. Used by permission of the publisher.

martyrs, saints, but also in the lives of un-distinguished millions upon millions—and, please God, in some small degree in our own lives. For something of that marvelous love of Jesus, something of his divine self-giving, has found, and is always finding, ever new realization. That is why, as we think of the passion of Jesus, we bow our heads in rever-ent awe before the victorious manifestation of the way of God in His world. In the light that shines from the Cross we know that all genuine love, from a mother's love to a life laid down in a great cause, has everlasting significance as it is linked with the driving power, the dynamic reality, declared in the ceaseless ongoing of the universe and in the life and death and rising again of Jesus Christ—the loving, untiring energy of the will of God.

The revelation, then, of what ultimate reality is, and of what God is doing in His world, is supremely given in the life and death of Jesus. It is well to insist upon the term "life," for in our concentration upon the last words of our Lord's earthly ministry we may all too easily fail to keep in mind the years of loving obedience to his Father.

In his dying upon the cross there came to sublime fulfillment all the meaning of the life of One who, born of a woman, born under the law, accepted to the full the vicissitudes, the ups and downs, of our human existence.

And his "tender words," as life ebbed, greatly help us to an understanding of that meaning because they let us see into the heart of the Christ. These utterances well up from the very depths of his being; they are a revelation of his inmost life. They were not said with deliberate intention to edify those who heard them. Each of these sayings was the instinctive response of his whole being to each situation as it developed.

In his last hours of intensified awareness he faced the elemental realities with which everyone is confronted: relationships of different kinds with other people, the doubt that comes very close to despair, the mystery of pain, the meaning of life and of death. And he dealt with them all in the power of his union with his Father's righteous, loving will. Since the whole of his earthly life had been lived in constant willing response to all that his Father might call upon him to do or to suffer, so, at the last, there was no merely passive resignation to what could not be escaped but the positive acceptance of all that might befall him, in the unfailing conviction that, in and through it all, his Father's will was to be done.

It was his, then, to have his part and place in the fulfillment of his Father's loving purpose. And so power streamed through him, power that makes of his dealing with those around him at the end and of his facing life's deepest problems, the means for a full revelation of what God's righteousness and love are accomplishing in this world. It is power to which we may relate our lives if, seeking to discern, in all the varied circumstances of daily living, the movement of God's will, we, in turn, open our hearts to the onflowing of his loving energy. And we find that the power that thus lays hold of us takes us deeper into life, brings us to closer grips with its problems and its difficulties and, it may be, asks of us unlooked for effort and sacrifice. But in the strength that the Christ gives, we shall discover that, through the very strains and tensions of life's demands, we are brought to new richness of living in constant awareness of God's inexhaustible giving of Himself to us, His children.

Almighty God, whose most dear Son went not up to joy but first he suffered pain, and entered not into glory before he was crucified; Mercifully grant that we, walking in the way of the cross, may find it none other than the way of life and peace; through the same thy Son Jesus Christ our Lord. Amen.

Two

And when they were come to the place which is called Calvary, there they crucified him and the malefactors, one on the right hand and the other on the left. Then said Jesus, Father, forgive them for they know not what they do.

—LUKE 23:33,34

$\mathcal{F}$ather, for-
give them." That is the one petition that
Jesus makes in these last hours; all his desire
is gathered up into this one prayer. The
longing for this forgiveness of human sin
was a prevailing passion in the heart of the
Christ. He began his teaching with the call
to repentance as a prelude to the receiving
of forgiveness. In the early days of his ministry they had brought him a paralytic lying
upon a bed, and the healing of the poor
man's infirmity began as Jesus looked at him
and said, "Son, thy sins be forgiven thee."
In the Parable of the Prodigal Son as the
father runs to meet the lad returning from
his wayward course, we rightly feel that we
are close to the very essence of Jesus' teaching about God's forgiving love. And here,
in the suffering and death of our Lord, we
are again face to face with what that forgiveness costs.

But we can understand how terrible the
cost must inevitably be only as we really

take to heart what sin really means. For sin is preeminently that which separates, that which shuts one in on one's self. There is always something of a sense of loneliness that follows the doing of what we know to be wrong. We realize this especially when we have wronged one for whom we really care. Though our friend may not be aware of what we have done, we feel that a barrier has been interposed between him and some part of ourselves. We cannot respond to his friendship as we did before. How much more, as we think of our relationship to God, does the sense of separation make itself felt. We are, as it were, out of touch with life; that is to say, out of loving relationship to that enveloping and pervading energy of God's self-giving by which life is constantly communicated to us and sustained. We are thrown back upon ourselves, living upon our own meager resources.

Yet the fact is there. The sin committed, the self-centered attitude taken, is part of the record. There is no getting back to the point where it had not happened. But in forgiveness the flooding power of God's love breaks through the barrier, and catches us up out of our self-imprisonment, into new relationship to His own streaming life. Forgiveness is not just a suspending of sentence, a remission of penalty, a willingness upon God's part to overlook the past. It is the communication of new life, the restoration of fellowship with the source of all life.

And here is the marvelous thing that God's creative and redemptive power does. It takes the very weakness, the failure, even the deliberate rebellion of which we have been guilty, and makes them the means by which we are drawn into closer relationship to Himself with a deeper understanding of life's meaning and the part and place He would have us take in it. The wretched misdirection of energies that our sin represented is now seen to be the perversion of gifts that our Father has bestowed upon us, and we find our joy in the realization that these misused powers may find their true and glad employment in His service.

It is out of the inexhaustible abundance of God's creative energy that the power to forgive comes so that in the everflowing stream of His love even the past can be transfigured. ⟩ So a poet of recent times can write:

25

And we that have most greatly sinned
Can least of all afford
To lose one fraction of redeeming love.
Rather let all the past
Purged of its bitterness fear and strife
Enrich the pattern woven for us above
And serve to deepen that abundant life
He gives to His beloved.[1]

But this redeeming energy is brought to
bear upon the human scene and enters into
the very depths of human living only because, in the person of Jesus Christ, God has
made Himself one with struggling, pitifully
failing mankind, meeting it at its point of
direst extremity, Himself accepting the worst
that sin can do.

This is what Good Friday means: *God in
Christ reconciling the world unto Himself,
not from outside as if just stooping down
from above but from within the process of
human life, charging it with strange, new
possibilities of achievement. And the identification of the Son of God with this life of
ours comes to its completion as death itself*

[1] E. S. Barlow, *Return and Other Poems* (Lon-
don: Grant Richards, 1924).

*is made the means by which He penetrates
to the very heart of human existence.*

The glorious life of God in Jesus Christ
through that dying upon the cross, before
which we bow today in reverent remem-
brance, is still carrying forward its work of
redeeming man from the pitiful plight in
which sin has involved him, still bringing
new vision of life's meaning and new power
to translate that vision into the terms of
human living as we discover what forgiveness means. A great European philosopher
of the last generation, whose unfaltering
quest of truth has set its stamp upon much
of the philosophic outlook of our own day,
had long been drawn towards acceptance of
the Christian faith, but had been held back
by over-scrupulous intellectual questioning.
But in his last illness he was heard to ex-
claim, "What a wonderful day! Good Friday! Christ has forgiven us everything." So
at every Eucharist we commemorate the
"one full, perfect, and sufficient sacrifice, ob-
lation, and satisfaction, for the sins of the
whole world." And it is ours to know this
forgiveness in our own lives, to find ourselves
released from the burden of our self-center-

27

edness; and taken up into the encompassing tide of our Lord's redeeming energy, it is ours to live in him and his to live in us.

It is in the light of this relationship to the Christ that we can understand the meaning of the indissoluble connection between God's forgiveness of us and our forgiveness of those who have wronged us. "If ye forgive not men their trespasses, neither will your Father forgive your trespasses." God's love, shed abroad in our hearts, cannot have its way with us to do all that forgiveness means in the communication of new life if we do not let it take us into the heart of His love for His world. That inevitably includes a love for those who have hurt us and wronged us, a love which will find its own expression in our attitude toward them. This readiness upon our part to forgive may not at once bring about the restoration of fellowship, that taking them back into our lives which is the fulfillment of forgiveness; but it will mean that our power in Christ of forgetting self, in imaginative understanding of the lives of others, will prepare the way for genuine reconciliation when the time comes. Meanwhile, our hearts will, in all sincerity, go out to them. Each of us as we have received forgiveness must be, in his own sphere, a center of reconciliation as Christ himself is in the whole world.

On the cross, then, our Lord draws us into unison with his own redeeming power so that his grace can flow into all the relationships of our lives. That is why the admonition in the Epistle to the Ephesians makes no impossible demand upon us: "Be ye kind one to another, tenderhearted, forgiving one another, even as God for Christ's sake hath forgiven you." This admonition is addressed, in the first instance, to those who have been baptized into the fellowship of the Church. But if we members of the Church would only rise obediently to the full realization of what it means to be members of the Society of the Forgiven, the Church would be enabled to minister so much more richly to the world at large the grace of reconciliation.

And it is that grace—God in the Church bringing the world back to Himself—that, in a human society in which fear, misunderstanding, contempt, and hatred so largely prevail, can break down prejudice and overcome estrangements and hostility. So it can bring to pass ultimate victory of the goodness of God, which from the cross is foreshadowed, here and now in the forgiveness of sins. In that reconciliation we are called to play our part, in union with our Lord.

O Lord our God, open our hearts, we pray thee, to the inflowing of thy forgiving love. Break down, we beseech thee, the barriers of self-satisfaction that separate us from sharing in thy all conquering life. Enable us in the power of thy self-giving to live generously, ready to forgive others even as thou hast forgiven us for the sake of him, who died upon the cross that we might live, our Lord and Saviour Jesus Christ. Amen.

Three

Verily I say unto thee, Today shalt thou be with me in paradise.

—LUKE 23:43

$\mathcal{S}$o the Christ with royal tenderness meets the touching cry of the penitent malefactor, "Jesus, remember me when thou comest into thy kingdom." "Verily I say unto you," he responds (to paraphrase his words), "I pledge you my word today you shall be with me in paradise. You shall have your part and place in my life beyond death." The poor lost criminal whose hand had been against every man's, who in his last moment had turned to ask for the consideration he had disdained in the past, was assured of companionship with the Lord of life.

How wonderfully characteristic of our Lord's earthly ministry is this crowning deed of mercy. He said that he had come to seek and to save that which was lost. He was the friend of publicans and sinners. He was charged with too frequent association with them. But he did not simply know in general that they needed him. His love went out to meet each individual that sought him at that individual's particular point of need. So in the young man who had kept all the commandments of the law from his youth up, he could see possibilities of heroic achievement and he bade him, "Go, sell all that thou hast and give to the poor and come follow me." On the other hand, the despised little tax-gatherer, Zaccheus, who in a burst of generous repentance, cried, "Behold, the half of my goods I give to the poor," receives the blessing: "Today is salvation come to this house."

Or again we see Jesus on the way to Jerusalem with that about his bearing which spoke of stern resolution to carry through an appointed task, no matter what the cost. His disciples, as they followed him, were bewildered and dismayed. As he passed through Jericho a blind man sitting by the wayside hailed him with the cry, "Jesus, thou son of David, have mercy upon me." There were many who sought to silence this intruder, but Jesus himself had the man brought to him and healed the man of his blindness. His concentration on the crisis in his ministry that lay before him could not make him less sensitive to the cry of need from the wayside. And even so, Jesus upon his cross is sensitively responsive to the pathetic longing of the man beside him to be remembered.

It has been well said that Christianity's greatest single contribution to forming the imagination and, therefore, the moral tradition of Europe (the western world) has been the idea of mercy which arises directly from the theology of redemption. Ordinarily, we hardly realize that it is from the Christ upon his cross that there has sprung the deep-seated and widespread conviction that the poor, the weak, the helpless, have an indefeasible claim upon human effort to remedy their distress. It is this conviction that finds expression in all the varied forms of community service. Whatever may be the yet unsolved problems associated with the welfare state, we are bound to acknowledge that it is one of the ways in which the profound truth, that the need of any is the concern of all, is finding practical expression. On the larger field there is the world-wide activity of the Red Cross with its significantly Christian name. There is the generous outpouring of many millions in world relief, and that not only on the part of a prosperous people such as ours.

We, who rejoice to call ourselves Christians, are glad to participate in all this and to feel that we do it in the name of our Lord and so have some part in his work of redeeming love. But in a day like this, when our thoughts are centered on what redemption costs in the agony and dying of the compassionate Christ, we may well ask ourselves whether we have quite accepted all that participation in our Lord's redeeming work really means. Is there not always the possibility that in making our contribution or rendering our service, whatever it may be, we do it as those who stretch out the helping hand from the vantage point of a kind of privileged position or from that of generous, but detached, onlookers? Perhaps the test of our inmost feeling for others lies in our attitude toward those with whom in daily life we are brought into immediate contact.

The founder of the first school of social work in England, who can hardly be charged with failure to appreciate the worth of organized community service, has emphatically said, "No available skill exists which can take the place of the all-powerful influence of human sympathy, neighbor interest, and the affection which true *caritas* involves." He uses the word *caritas* because of the difficulty of finding an English equivalent for the Greek word *agape*—charity, or love, as our versions render it. There is that tremendous saying of St. Paul: "Though I bestow all my goods to feed the poor, and though I give my body to be burned, and have not charity, it profiteth me nothing."

Jesus upon his cross, responding to the deepest need of the man by his side, gives the supreme revelation of what *caritas,* charity or love, means. His very suffering can render him so deeply sensitive to the piteous craving of a soul for simple recognition, because throughout his ministry he identified himself so completely with the human struggle. And as we are taken up into the stream of his redeeming life, we must go with him into the depth of the human tragedy with all its aching effort, and so share within that struggle our Lord's compassionate understanding of man's need and aspirations as

37

they meet us in the lives of those with whom we have to do in the day by day business of living.

Life brings to all of us, as it brought to Jesus, much unsought companionship. An attitude of indifference is perhaps the easiest course to adopt towards people with whom our own daily round of duty involves us, especially when there is that about them which is, to say the least, uncongenial. But participation in our Lord's redeeming love takes us, at some cost, undoubtedly, deeper into life so that we see each individual, as it were, in the round, in his likeness to ourselves and his distinctive difference from us. What we may, at times, be tempted to regard only as an intolerable self-seeking, is felt to be, in part, the expression of that same energy that surges within us, a reaching after a more abundant life which we, for our part, gratefully acknowledge is given us in union with the life of our Lord. So we may "see into the depths of human souls, souls that appear to have no depth at all to careless eyes." That does not mean, of course, that we are to exercise any intrusive interest in the lives of those about us. Far from that, in our awareness of the sacred reality of each inner life, we shall shrink from any undue encroachment upon it.

Yet, in our dealings with others, there will always be a note of courtesy—that grace so strangely lacking in these days when so much is said about the worth of the individual. Sometimes, too, it will be given us, in our sympathy with life in all its manifestations, by simple instinctive look or gesture, to make things, for the moment, at any rate, a little brighter for someone who finds it hardgoing. And then, every now and again, there will come the time when someone by our side, in great need, will turn to us, and by wont of our continued striving to live in the power of our Lord's self-sacrificing love, we shall be quick to hear and answer. So it may be ours, perhaps, at much cost, with glad heart, to provide just that answer to human need that shall give new strength and courage to the life of another.

Jesus, in his dying hour, taking the penitent thief into new relationship to himself, has given new and exacting, but rewarding, meaning to the great commandment, "Thou shalt love thy neighbor as thyself."

Blessed Lord, who for our sakes didst take upon thee our nature and dost know in thine own person our human need and aspiration: Enable us, we beseech thee in the power of thy love, to see thee in the lives of those about us and be ever ready to minister to their need as thou shalt grant us opportunity. We ask it in thy name, who with the Father and the Holy Spirit livest and reignest ever, one God, world without end. Amen.

Four

When Jesus, therefore, saw his mother, and the disciple standing by, whom he loved, he saith unto his mother, Woman, behold thy son. Then saith he to the disciple, Son, behold thy mother.

—JOHN 19:26,27

$\mathcal{H}$ow simply and naturally amid all the strain and anguish of these last hours can our Lord forget self and enter into the heart of his mother and of his closest friend, feeling intensely what the pain of separation from one they so dearly love must mean to them. The life of Jesus was knit, as ours, into the ties of love and friendship. He knew the joy of happy companionship with those for whom he greatly cared. We think of him in the home of Martha and Mary: Mary listening to him talk while Martha is busy providing refreshments, and we hear his gentle affectionate reply to Martha's complaint that she has all the work to do.

Many such moments of quiet enjoyment there must have been in the life of Jesus, and it is well to think of these because, in our very right desire to acknowledge to the full the divinity of our Lord, it is all too easy to forget that he was also completely one with us in our human nature, sin only excepted, very God *and* very man. So it would sometimes seem as if his presence here upon earth is thought of as simply that of one commissioned to carry through a difficult task which he wanted to be done with as soon as possible. True enough, he entered into the heart of the human struggle. He knew hardship and weariness. Often he had not where to lay his head.

But he entered into the joy of human living, too. He loved this dear familiar earth of ours. The great saying, "Consider the lilies of the field, how they grow; they toil not, neither do they spin: And yet I say unto you, That even Solomon in all his glory was not arrayed like one of these," could have been uttered only by one who had felt and rejoiced in the loveliness of the flowers. And the parables reflect not only his loving observation of the life-giving processes of nature, but also a delight in the interesting, and sometimes odd, ways of human beings.

It is perhaps particularly worthwhile in these days to dwell upon this relation of the divine life to the positive values in the life of man. In a world in which so much seems hopelessly wrong, in which men face the sad wreckage of human hope that greed and the lust for power can bring about, and in which hatred and fear seem to be the dominant forces, inevitably it is out of their pitiful need and failure, and out of their desperate realization that they have no power of themselves to help themselves, that men turn to the God of all power and wisdom for deliverance.

And here, as we are meditating upon our Lord's identification of himself, even to the acceptance of ignominious death with human need and suffering, and as we try to realize anew that it is the outpouring of his life upon the cross that has given to us, who have so often sinned against his love, a renewal of life in union with himself, we may, indeed, believe that, through all the strain and stress, God is at work within His world, calling men back to the acknowledgment of His righteousness and His love. We may, indeed, rejoice in the return to religion that is undoubtedly showing itself in many quarters, while we ask ourselves whether we, too, are not being summoned to a deeper understanding of the way in which God in Christ, at infinite cost to Himself, seeks to redeem His children from the dire consequences of their self-will.

But at the same time we must never forget that the God who thus redeems is the God who has brought this wonderful world into being, has given us life and sustains us every moment of our existence. More than that, He has endowed us with distinctive gifts of mind and feeling, as well as the freedom to use them as we will. All the amazing capacity for human achievement stands in direct relationship to the life of God Himself, and this achievement is still going forward.

For example, if indeed the thought of the atom today calls up, first of all, the awful means of destruction which man has devised for himself, that thought must not stand in the way of an awed recognition of the revelation of the divine energy stored up in the atom, a revelation for which human research has prepared the way. We must recognize too, the greatness of God's gift of intellectual ability that through its age-long exercise has prepared the way for this amazing release of power. It is the misuse of God's gifts that has brought tragedy and cries out for redemption.

And of all the gifts that God has given to man, there is none greater than the power to love, to go out of self into the lives of others, to feel the mystery and the amazing worth of their being, and to long for the will and the ability to count for good in their life. In a diffused form, this power is responsible for all sorts and kinds of human association, from the nation down to the little group of intimates who meet often just for the pleasure of being together. It is not good that man should be alone, was the divine pronouncement when man was created. But, of course, this linking of life with life manifests itself supremely in the relationship of the family, of husband and wife, of parents and children, and every now and again, in the ties of intimate friendship.

Jesus gave new depth of meaning to these relationships. His loving entering into the joys and problems of childhood has invested the bond between mother and child with a new sacredness. At the time when there had begun to dawn in him the consciousness of a mysterious destiny in relationship to his Father in heaven, he went down to Nazareth with his parents and was subject to them, and his mother kept all these sayings in her heart. There is the lad, with his own distinctive course of life opening before him and with a new power within him that presses for utterance, quietly awaiting the further revelation of God's will as he may find it in the demands and privileges of the home, while his mother cherishes humbly in her heart the strange signs of that otherness in her child's life that is to take him from her. How wonderful is the portrayal of the Holy Family in which artists have delighted as they picture the mother bending over the babe in adoring love, tinged with resigned foreboding of what the future may hold in store, while in the background Joseph provides a sturdy assurance of affectionate support and care.

And on the cross in the dreadful fulfillment of that destiny dimly foreshadowed from the first, Jesus brings the tenderest ties that knit human lives together face to face with that which so terribly seems to threaten their very existence and meaning—separation, death, and bereavement. Because his love for his mother and his friend has absolutely no note of selfishness in it, he can, in utter self-forgetfulness, become part of the unique fulfillment of their future as he gives his final benediction, "Woman, behold thy son. Son, behold thy mother." Always in days to come, in the happiness of the companionship in which they rejoice, they knew him present, still the object of their love and adoration.

Now it is the redemption of that wonderful human power to love that takes place upon the cross. So in our Lord's loving self-forgetfulness, free of all that possessiveness which so easily creeps into our care for our dear ones, this power to love is set always in relationship to the will of God, and so receives an everlasting reality of which death itself can only unfold the deeper meaning.

It is seeing those we love in the light of the divine life that sustains them, of the divine love that would have them grow into ever richer employment of the gifts of mind and heart that it has bestowed upon them, that can enable us to enter into the fullness of all that our relationship to them may mean. It is so easy to have good, general ideas of what being a husband or a wife, a father, a mother, a son or daughter, ought to mean, and miss the particular and unique note that such a relationship in any given case demands. Unconsciously we fill these general ideas with our own self-esteem, instead of learning from what those who are near to us do for us and expect of us, instead of seeking that richer understanding of human relationship which God would have us seek. One thinks of a father who is blind to his son's deepest aspiration because he cannot reconcile it with his own preconceived idea of what a son ought to be; or of husbands and wives who miss the full unfolding of the marriage relationship; because each has an unchangeable definition of what that relationship ought to be, they cannot enter together upon the discovery of the new values which God would make known to them through their life together.

If it is really the doing of God's will to which our lives are actually committed, and not merely the hallowing of our own self-interest, then in and through the tender relationships of family life and intimate friendships, we shall increasingly be drawn to deeper joy in the surrender of self, even if it be at times very costly. So we shall be taken into closer participation in the life of the Christ and in him into deathless union with those we dearly love.

O Lord Jesus Christ, who on thy cross didst take loving thought for thy Mother and thy friend: Grant us grace to be always tender and thoughtful in our relations with those who are near and dear to us. Give us, we beseech thee, in our home and in our friendships, powers of understanding and sympathy, that through us there may be shed abroad something of thine own divinely human love. We ask it in thy name, who with the Father and the Holy Ghost livest and reignest, One God, world without end. Amen.

Five

And at the ninth hour Jesus cried with a
loud voice, saying, ELOI, ELOI, LAMA SABACH-
THANI? which is, being interpreted, My God,
my God, why hast thou forsaken me?

—MARK 15:34

*T*his passionate cry of despair ringing through the darkness startles us. It is a cry of terrible bereavement and unutterable loneliness.

Knowing what we do of the life of Jesus, of its close and intimate communion with God, of the calm confidence with which he had faced hardship and suffering, the hatred and the scorn of men, and thinking as we do of the quiet figure, serene and strong, before Caiaphas, the high priest, and Pilate, the Roman governor, to us this cry of abandonment seems all the more heartbreaking.

It is, perhaps, significant of the effect upon those who heard it that this is the one word from the cross that has been handed down, not simply in a translation into Greek, but in the original Aramaic that Jesus spoke. The syllables *Eloi Eloi lama sabachthani* are just those which fell from Jesus' lips as, for the moment, he found himself sinking into the abyss of nothingness and knowing that sense of the utter meaninglessness of life, that sense of blank despair that is the most terrifying experience a man can be called upon to face, far worse than death itself. In entering into this life of ours to be one with us, he must penetrate to the very heart of human distress: he must know what it is to feel that there is just no way out; that one is caught, as it were, in a trap, with no one to turn to for help and with nothing worth doing if one could, for there is no one that cares; and when all is said and done, what can one's little ego count for over against the vast heedless process of the universe.

For Jesus, life's meaning was to be found in doing his Father's will. That had meant carrying on his ministry of love, of healing the sick, restoring sight to the blind, bringing to the down-and-out a message of hope and of restoration, being, in fact, the means through which his Father's love exercised its creative redeeming power in the midst of human life. In exercising that ministry, he had known the exhaustion that giving so generously of himself to human need must necessarily involve. There had been times when he had indeed felt that power had gone out of him. He had been weary and heavy laden, but it had been sheer joy, for he had come, not to do his own will, but the will of his Father. And this self-commitment of Jesus meant the continued response of his heart to the Father's will as it was gradually revealed in the day by day course of events.

The very greatness of our belief in Jesus as the only begotten Son of God—with what we feel to be the perfect relationship of love between God the Father and God the Son —sometimes leads us to forget that that relationship found its complete expression in the terms of finite human experience with all its limited view of the future and with the necessity of waiting patiently, at times, upon the disclosure of God's will. It was under such conditions that Jesus knew the wonder of standing in a relationship of love to the God of infinite power and wisdom, whose might held the vast universe in being; that he knew the wonder of the fact that his own brief years of existence were in unceasing life-giving contact with the ultimate reality which, underneath all the strange sequence of change and decay that characterizes the

earthly scene, knows no ending—the will
of the God of everlasting beauty and goodness.

It was the awareness of this relationship
in his day by day experience that had sustained him as he moved forward to the inevitable end upon the cross. This had enabled him to utter the prayer that his Father
would forgive those who were putting him
to death, to give new hope to the dying thief,
to bestow blessing upon mother and friend;
and then as the darkness gathered, there was
nothing more to be done and, with his look
turned inward, he felt himself for the moment just a passive, helpless victim, ending
his life in failure.

In the utter loneliness of his spirit, it
seemed as if even the God to whom his life
had been so completely committed, was for-
saking him. But still there was the unshake-
able certainty that God was there, even in
the darkness, and so the cry that forced itself to his lips was not simply a cry of despair. It was an appeal to One who, though
for the time being strangely hidden, was
nonetheless declaring Himself with power
even in the mysterious act of withdrawal,

One whom he could still name "My God"
and of whom he could ask, "Why?"

It is, then, never to be forgotten that there
was a time when Jesus, in his complete sharing in our human experience, had to commit
himself to One, the movement of whose will
he could not, for the moment, understand, so
that he must lay his despairing doubt before
a God hidden in the darkness.

It would, of course, be a mistaken reading
of our times to think of the widely prevailing pessimism of our day as growing out of
a conviction that God has abandoned His
world, that, in Nietzsche's startling phrase,
"God is dead." Great numbers of men of
good will who have dedicated themselves to
the services of good causes—the cause of
world-wide peace, of freedom for all, of a
life for everyone without material anxiety—
have not thought of their devotion as given
to the God whose love is constantly seeking
to bestow new and richer life on all His children. So when these causes have seemed well-
nigh doomed to failure, these men have not
felt that intensity of anguish that men feel
when the personal relationship with One to
whom they have wholly given themselves

seems to have been dissolved and life itself seems to have played them false. Sadly enough, they have not thought of God as involved to that degree in our human struggle.

Even within the Church we are not often sufficiently aware that the very meaning of the Church's life, its sacraments, its creeds, its concern for conduct, is that through it all we are being brought into relationship to the living God, whose love is continually searching us out to draw us into, and hold us in, union with Himself. And so we do not feel that in the Church's failure God's own love is involved even though, at times, it seems to have withdrawn itself from His world. But, nonetheless, although God be not called in question, there is today among people who really care, both within the Church and in the world at large, a wide-spread feeling that, behind the seeming defeat of so much that might make for the good life for all, there is something wrong with life itself. So there is in many souls a tragic failure of belief in life; and behind their lack of belief in life there is ultimately, though it may not so name itself, lack of belief in God. The last few decades have seen such appalling world-wide tragedy, have seen such devastating destruction not only of material goods but of traditional ways of thinking and relationships of trust, that we are sometimes tempted to feel that life itself is bankrupt; but such thinking would really mean that God had abandoned His world, or (if we think in the terms of our religion) that God has come in dreadful judgment. Indeed, at such moments, we forget that God's judgment is a prelude to redemption and, therefore, even through what seems only destruction, He is working out His great purpose for His world. To quote Tennyson's lines:

Power is with us in the night
Which makes the darkness and the light
And dwells not in the light alone.

The world remains God's world, and we may cry, "*My* God," if only we are ready, in the shadow of the darkness that shrouds the cross and in the power that streams from it, to put ourselves unreservedly in His hands, even though for the time being the meaning of what He is doing in His world is hidden from us. That does not mean that we shall not devote the best of thought and effort that we can command to the solution of the problems that confront us, but always we shall know that our thought and effort are to be used as God wills in the carrying out of His infinite purpose of love far transcending our limited understanding—a purpose of love that is giving and will give far more than we desire or deserve.

All this holds true, too, of our own personal lives. There come times when, in the face of overwhelming difficulty or apparently hopeless failure, we feel that life has lost its meaning; and in the degree that we have been trying to serve God faithfully, we are hopelessly at a loss, because it is God Himself that has seemed to fail us. "Why," we say, "should this happen to me? Does God really care?"

If we can only remember that just as for every breath we draw, we are dependent upon His sustaining energy, so too the power to question, even to doubt, comes from Him, we shall then know that our very capacity to feel intensely is telling us that we are still in His hands and that, though *we* cannot see the meaning of it all, there is undoubtedly His meaning for our lives; and we shall hold fast to the certainty that, by what He has done for us in the past, He has shown Himself to be indeed our God; we shall know, too, that He to whom all hearts are open, all desires known, will tenderly discern in our cry of passionate, despairing sincerity the depth of our craving for Him; and we shall find new courage in the conviction that in the mystery of His loving will lies our ultimate peace and joy.

O God, who in the mystery of Thy love, didst suffer Thy dear Son to feel forsaken of Thee: Grant us in all our doubts the rememberance of Thy goodness; in the darkness the awareness of Thy glory though we cannot behold it; the loving acceptance of the duty immediately at hand though we cannot see beyond it; and so bring us at last to the clear vision of Thyself; through the same Thy Son Jesus Christ, our Lord. Amen.

Six

After this, Jesus knowing that all things were now accomplished, that the scripture might be fulfilled, saith, I thirst.

—JOHN 19:28

$\mathcal{T}$his simple statement of Jesus gathers up into itself all the agony of the fevered body and the parched throat and the tortured limbs. There are forms of artistic representation of the crucifixion which seem to dwell morbidly upon the physical suffering which the victim must undergo; and, perhaps, in reaction from these we are tempted unconsciously to turn our minds away from consideration of the intensity of actual physical pain which such a death meant. Yet we dare not forget that, in his dying upon the cross, the poor racked frame of the Lord Jesus was called upon to undergo as painful a death as human brutality could devise, and that he suffered as only a sensitively organized body could suffer when exposed to rude torture.

Yet, there is no suggestion of complaint about his utterance but rather a quiet acceptance of suffering, for the words, "I thirst," are just a simple statement of his need and of his readiness to receive such help as a bystander could give. So he moistened his lips and throat with the vinegar and water which a rough soldier offered him on a sponge.

It is perhaps significant that these three last sayings from the cross that fall so close together as the end comes and breathe a spirit of quiet acceptance, follow upon the cry of spiritual agony which we have just considered. It would seem that having descended into the depths and there, at the heart of the bitter loneliness, having found Him to whom he could cry, "My God," Jesus felt that the worst was over; and in the conviction that nothing could separate him from his Father's love, he began to find rest and peace as death drew near.

In these days we have learned much about the relationship between the spiritual and the physical. Our wisest psychiatrists have insisted that the source of much of our physical disability is to be found, in no small degree, in a disintegration of our inner life; or, quite simply, that in time of illness what is called the "emotional factor" plays an immensely important role. What many a psychiatrist also has discovered is that it is only as the patient feels that he can draw upon resources from beyond himself that he knows himself to be in touch with reality, and that true integration of the self can be brought about.

And the reality with which we, who are trying to be followers of Jesus Christ, know our lives to be in touch is none other than the power and might of the living God, but it is power and might that has subdued itself to the weakness of the Cross and has thus entered into the heart of human suffering and sorrow and made weakness, and suffering, and sorrow, the means by which new beauty, new splendor, new joy, has enriched human existence.

This participation of the divine life in the dread actuality of pain and suffering that all men at some time or another have to experience, does not indeed explain that pain and suffering, for the mystery lies beyond our human understanding. The Cross, however, has wrought a significant change in our attitude toward pain and suffering, for the Cross strips it of that dreadful sense of isolation that can add so grievously to suffering, both physical and mental, that feeling that one is shut in upon one's self and called upon, strangely, to endure what no one else can understand. The realization that in pain and sorrow the divine life itself is striving within us and drawing us into union with our Lord means that we feel, even as we suffer, that ours is not a separate experience, but that we share in the massive movement of the world's pain and grief by which God's own purpose of redemption for His children is being fulfilled. We think of St. Paul's words, "That I may know him, and the power of his resurrection, and the fellowship of his sufferings, being made conformable unto his death."

We may contrast this sense of a fellowship of suffering in Christ with a very different way of regarding the sufferings of others; with, for example, the Greek attitude, which could go no further than ask, in the words of Euripides, "Why should men be repelled by one another's sufferings." We can then understand why it is that, under Christian auspices, there grew up the grave concern for the weak and helpless, the sad and the suffering, that finds expression in countless ways of ministering to their needs. It is not strange that in the light of the Christian faith, on the one hand, our occasion for suffering is increased because our awareness of the way in which our life is bound up with all men is profoundly deepened, though, on the other hand, new insistence is laid on seeking, in every possible way, to alleviate pain and to relieve suffering by the work of physicians and nurses and by the understanding sympathy of wise counsellors. For when all allowance is made for other factors that have played their part in the increasing provision of tender care for the sick and helpless, it still remains true that the great saying of Jesus, "I was sick and ye visited me. . . . Inasmuch as ye have done it unto one of the least of these my brethren, ye have done it unto me," has set, from the very beginning, the note of truly Christian practice.

Yet all the time there remains the consciousness of the inevitability of pain and grief that must be borne. But with the deeper understanding that profound sympathy has brought, there has come the belief that through these also the creative will of God is at work, bringing new values into this life of ours. We can feel this when we think of the way in which art has depicted human life, as, for example, in the contrast between the untroubled physical perfection of a Greek statue and the living intensity of Michael Angelo's David or in the strange sense of spiritual power that speaks through the harassed, and it may be, wasted countenance of a Rembrandt portrait. Through the tensions of soul and body a secret power, the power of One who triumphed through suffering and death, can transform sorrow and pain into new greatness and richness of living in relationship to the God of life and love. So a Belgian poet, bereaved of a dearly loved son, can write:

> *Joy and pain are complementary. We must enjoy life to realize its value, but we must suffer to understand its meaning. There is something beyond joy and pain, including both, transcending both.*

So, perhaps, in time of sore distress we, too, may have turned our hearts Godward and found ourselves, not indeed at once freed from pain and anxiety, but given strength to carry on, and more than that, to feel that through it all we have been taken into a deeper understanding of the way in which life moves on to ever greater worth and meaning. If this has not as yet been our own experience, we can hardly have failed to see it in the lives of others—perhaps of someone very dear to us, of someone who has not simply borne up under prolonged illness that involved almost constant pain, but has been able to give strength and courage to others with a wonderful breadth of sympathy and loving understanding of their problems and difficulties. Power has thus flowed into life from him, who on the bitter cross accepted pain and suffering in fulfillment of his Father's loving will.

O Lord Jesus Christ, who in thy passion hast sounded the depths of human anguish: Grant, we beseech thee, that in all we are called upon to bear of pain physical or mental, we may be drawn into the fellowship of thy sufferings and so into deeper sympathy with the pain and grief of others and into a new sense of union with thy redeeming love. We ask it in thy name, who with the Father and the Holy Ghost livest and reignest ever, one God, world without end. Amen.

Seven

When Jesus therefore had received the vinegar, he said, It is finished.

—JOHN 19:30

*T*his cry of Jesus is not just one of relief, as if he were thankful that life's sorrowful journey was at an end. The Greek word "finished" means not simply "over and done with," but "brought to a complete fulfillment." It corresponds to a saying found in our Lord's great high priestly prayer, "I have finished the work which thou gavest me to do."

How strange this almost joyous word of fulfillment must have sounded in the ears of those who were standing by, especially of those who, like the priests and Pharisees, had followed the ministry of Jesus with hostile intent. For here was a young man who had not reached what we think of today as the prime of life, coming, apparently, to an untimely end in the company of criminals, and yet, with his dying breath, declaring that he was content because he had fulfilled his life's destiny.

We, who know that the course of the world was changed because Jesus lived those brief years among men and died upon a cross, bow in reverent awe before the glorious perfection of a life that came to so marvelous completion. We cannot find ourselves thinking what he might have done if only he had been spared. It was all so inevitably right, the unity of life and death. "Ah, but," we say—and we here speak out of our own very devotion to our Lord, out of our grateful recognition of the life of God Himself revealed in him—"it was so simple a matter for him to carry through to its perfect fulfillment his life's work, for it had all been planned beforehand, and all he had to do, so to speak, was to carry out that which had been ordained." So once again we fail to take, with all its full meaning, our Lord's complete identification with our human struggle. He accepted all the responsibilities, perplexities, and anxieties that God's gift of freedom to His children carries with it. Like us, he had to make decisions in the face of changing conditions and opportunity. It was out of the ebb and flow of circumstance that he fashioned the pattern of the perfect life. We think of the temptations in the wilderness when, with a throbbing sense of extraordinary power seeking expression within him, he had to decide whether to use that power for the satisfaction of his own need and the enhancement of his own prestige and authority or to follow the way of humble self-sacrificing ministry and teaching.

There is a passage in the Epistle to the Hebrews that boldly declares, "Though he were a Son, yet learned he obedience by the things which he suffered." That is to say, in day by day experience he learned to discern what his Father's will for him was. Sometimes this was unspeakably hard. The cry from the depths of his being in Gethsemane, "O my Father, if it be possible, let this cup pass from me," tells us that, even as the crisis drew near, there was still a measure of uncertainty as to just how his Father's will for him was to be realized. He must wait upon the course of events, responding at every moment to that love for him and for the world that he knew God was manifesting in every situation.

As the years go by, and especially in these days of so much uncertainty, when it sometimes seems hardly worthwhile to make plans far ahead, do we not find ourselves asking what is the meaning of it all and, in particular, what is the meaning of our own life? Sometimes it would seem to consist in just doing one thing after another, dispersing our energy and interest in this direction and that, with no substantial achievement to show that we can think of as giving lasting significance to our existence. Or perhaps we have associated ourselves with some good cause and put time and thought and energy into contributing to its success, and then there come moments when we wonder if, after all, our contribution really amounts to much, or even whether, in view of the apparent collapse of so much on which we had always counted, any cause can have permanent value. Or again we may have set our hearts on some limited achievement that seemed to lie within our own powers, yet because of failure we now have a feeling of frustration, a sense of just being carried along against our own will, we know not whither. And even in the event of success, there is so often sad disillusionment, a feeling that, after all, success means little in the face of the fact that everything is subject to change and decay, including our own little transitory self.

One is reminded of the utterance of the distinguished poet, W. B. Yeats, who, in middle age, at a time when everything seemed to indicate success, could write: "I am sorrowful and disturbed when I think of all the books I have read and of all the nice words I have heard spoken and of all the anxiety I have given to parent and grand-parent, for all life weighed on the scales of my own life seems to me a preparation for something that never happened."

"All life weighed on the scales of my own life." How pervasive and persistent is the reference to one's own self as the standard by which life's meaning is to be measured. So hard is it to keep constantly before us the truth that life's meaning is not my mean-ing, but God's meaning. That is to say, my aspiration, my striving, is to have lasting worth as it is taken up and included in the movement of God's righteous loving will, the will that is ceaselessly at work in Jesus Christ for the redemption of the whole of human existence. What we do and are may have their part and place in God's seeking to bring all men into the fellowship, one with another, of His love. Ours may be the joy of participation in the endless life of our Lord that, by his dying upon the cross, has the power to transmute sorrow, pain, and failure, as well as achievement, into everlasting beauty and splendor.

To make the effort constantly in all the happenings of life, to yield ourselves to the loving energy of the will of God pressing in upon us, is indeed to bring all the best powers of mind and body to the performance of each task, to use all the ability that God gives us in the making of our plans, and then place our planning and our effort in His hands, not prescribing the use He is to make of them, but glad to trust His wisdom and His love in the assurance that in union with the life of His dear Son all that is good and true in our striving will be given lasting worth and our own being will find complete fulfillment.

Enable us, O Lord our God, so to seek in all the circumstances of daily living the doing of that which thou wouldst have us do that we may come at last to that distinctive fulfillment of our life's meaning that thou dost grant to everyone that loveth thee; through Jesus Christ our Lord. Amen.

Eight

Father, into thy hands I commend my spirit:
and having said thus, he gave up the ghost.
—LUKE 23:46

*A*nd so the end comes in an act of simple self-commitment into his Father's keeping. How natural and inevitable it seems that one whose whole life had been a constant response to his Father's will should, in the last moments, gladly yield himself to his Father's embrace. For the name "Father" takes us into the very heart of Jesus' teaching about the nature and being of God—a teaching embodied not only in language of wonderful simplicity but in a life.

Men of olden time had thought and spoken of the living God as Father, but they could not know the depth of meaning with which that name of God is charged, or feel the intimacy of the relationship of which it speaks, until these were revealed in the unique and perfect sonship of Jesus Christ. It was, to be sure, only in a mutual responsiveness that the profound and all-embracing nature of the love of Father and Son could be revealed. We think of Jesus' first recorded utterance, the lad's reply to Mary and Joseph who had sought him sorrowing, "Wist ye not that I must be about my Father's business?" It is important to note the word "must." His relationship to his Father is not felt as a matter of his own option. It is there as something given to which he must make response.

But his Father's will is not thought of as simply a divinely established order to which he must yield *blind* obedience. It was a felt, moving energy with which his life was bound up, so that he knew that it was in union with the activity of God, that the dawning powers and ideals of his youth were to go on to their fullest and richest realization. And it was his free response to a necessity, not over against him, but felt within him, as the energetic working of his Father's will that gave to his compassionate ministry such power to make men feel the marvelous reality of God's love for His children.

The sense of a divine pressure within him finds expression in a saying of his uttered early in his ministry: "I must preach the kingdom of God to other cities also, for therefore am I sent." And this consciousness of a constraining force is to be discerned not only at moments of crisis in his life, as in the cry, "I have a baptism [a baptism of suffering] to be baptised with, and how am I straitened till it be accomplished," but also in periods of his experience of waiting, as witnessed in his statement, "Howbeit I must go on my way today and tomorrow and the day following." It is this constant response to God's intimate relationship to the course of his life at every moment that enabled Jesus in the agony of Gethsemane, through the pain and agony of crucifixion, and at the moment of his dying, to commit himself unreservedly to the certainty of his Father's love. When we realize what that intimacy of the Father's relationship to that human life of our Lord meant, we escape from making the false distinction that is sometimes made between a stern righteousness of God the Father and the tender forgiving love of God the Son. God so loved the world that He gave His only begotton Son, but in that giving the Father's heart went with him, the Father's life was in him. And we come

back to that sublime saying of St. Paul:
"God in Christ, reconciling the world unto
himself"—at infinite cost.

So it is that in our Lord's complete identification of himself with our human striving,
even to the point of accepting in his own
person all the worst that that striving involves, we are brought to feel the reality of
God our Father's love, not only in all that
ministers to our well being, but also in life's
stern discipline. It is quite easy, as long as
all goes well, to maintain a faith in God's
goodness. Indeed, many of us can remember
an almost complacent acceptance, in days
gone by, of what was rather superficially
conceived as God's ordering of the world
with a view to insuring as wide a distribu-
tion of comfort as possible. But in the darker
days that have followed, it has been for
many of us a simple matter to recognize the
part that human selfishness and greed and
lust for power have played in the destruction
of so much that we cherished in the past
and in bringing us to a state of dread uncertainty as to what the future may hold in
store. But it has been only too easy to forget
that God is as surely at work now within the

process, as in days of old, and that, in and through the strain and stress of the present, a Father's love, as declared in our Lord's participation in this life of ours, is summoning us to new understanding and realization of life's possibilities in union with One who brings victory out of defeat, new glorious life out of death.

And this holds abundantly true of our own personal lives, also. To discern the presence and power of the living, loving God, not only at times when we rejoice in the happiness of a quiet ordered existence in which, within reasonable limits, we successfully arrange life as we would like to have it, but also to find the same living, loving God pressing in upon our lives at times when we feel checked and thwarted, and it may be, even brought to the edge of despair, is to be taken again into union with that life of our Lord which probes to the uttermost human failure and pain and sorrow and brings out of them a new richness and fullness of living, a joyous sense of being made participant in the creative and redemptive movement of the divine life itself.

It is ours, then, to think of the stern

necessities of life, as for example, the inevitable sequence of cause and effect in the world of nature, or the relentless onward movement of time that carries us irresistibly forward, as representing not the arbitrary promulgation of laws imposed from above, but some of the ways in which the very present power of God Himself is penetrating and embracing our lives. We can thus discern in the ways of nature a love that can be depended upon and, in the passage of time as life moves relentlessly on, God's loving creative energy, ceaselessly at work, bringing the new into being. So we, too, may come face to face with death—the last inexorable fact of death—knowing that here also the loving presence and power of the same God are to be found—God who in Christ, from within the process of dying, brings to birth new and abundant life that knows no end. We shall find new meaning in the words, "buried with him," as we pray that through the grave and gate of death we may pass to our joyful resurrection.

But let us not end in thinking of ourselves. Let us, rather, look again to the sublime figure of Jesus upon his cross and let us hear one of the greatest of his followers speak of Christ Jesus, "who, existing in the form of God, counted not the being on an equality with God a thing to be grasped, but emptied himself, taking the form of a servant, being made in the likeness of men and being found in fashion as a man, he humbled himself, becoming obedient even unto death, yea the death of the cross; wherefore also God highly exalted him and gave unto him a name which is above every name, that at the name of Jesus every knee should bow, of things in heaven and things on earth and things under the earth, and that every tongue confess that Jesus Christ is Lord, to the glory of God the Father."

In that confession let us find the peace and joy that pass all understanding.

Grant, we beseech thee, Almighty God, that like as we do believe thy only-begotten Son our Lord Jesus Christ to have ascended into the heavens; so we may also in heart and mind thither ascend, and with him continually dwell, who liveth and reigneth with thee and the Holy Ghost, one God, world without end. Amen.